Bullying

When Your Child is the Target

Love and Logic

by Charles Fay, Ph.D.

Love and Logic Institute, Inc.
2207 Jackson Street, Golden, CO 80401-2300
www.loveandlogic.com | 800-338-4065

First edition
First printing, 2016
Printed in the United States of America
ISBN 978-1-942105-21-3

Copyediting: Joyce M. Gilmour, Brooklyn, WI

Introduction

Does teasing end when kids graduate from elementary school? Does it stop when they move on from middle to high school? Does it magically disappear when we become adults? Or is it sadly true that most of us will encounter bullies throughout our lifetimes?

Because we can't ensure that the world will always be sweet and kind to our kids, common sense tells us that we ought to equip them with skills that allow them to cope with this sometimes less-than-considerate world. In the pages that follow, you'll learn how to empower your kids to handle, and overcome, bullying. Learn how to walk beside them as they move from the role of victim to victor.

Kylie's parents shared her story:

"It started in third grade when she began wearing glasses. Classmates called her 'four eyes' and other bad names that we can't repeat.

"By sixth grade, some of the girls were pushing her around in the halls and after school.

"Now they've started spreading vicious rumors about her online.

One girl even used a photo-editing program to paste Kylie's head on a woman's nude body. Now it's floating around the internet."

We know Kylie's story is a common one. It's an experience familiar to far too many children and teens. We also know the consequences can be tragic.

Bullying hurts.

It hurts our kids, and we hurt for them.

We want it to stop right now. We wish we could rid the world of such hateful behavior.

When their kids encounter tough challenges, parents tend to fall into one of three styles.

Drill sergeant parents simply tell their children what to think, feel, or do.

Drill sergeant parents say,...

"You shouldn't be so upset by those kids."
"You just need to remind yourself to be strong."
"You need to ignore them or tell your teacher."

Sometimes we have to tell our children what to do.

If we do it too often, however, will they get enough practice learning to solve the problems they face?

Telling strong-willed children what to do also lands us in plenty of arguments and power struggles.

Power struggles and arguments damage our relationships.

The unstated message sent by drill sergeant parents:

"You're not capable of thinking for yourself. I'll have to do it for you."

Parents who've overused the drill sergeant style often wonder why their teens have difficulty thinking for themselves in the face of peer pressure.

Helicopter parents consistently hover and rescue.

They frantically perform cartwheels and jump through hoops attempting to shield their children from all forms of disappointment, conflict, or struggle.

Helicopter parents make bullying and teasing a **bigger** problem for their kids.

Do children develop skills to avoid or resolve peer conflicts when they come to believe they will never have to?

Do they develop the mental toughness to deal with nasty characters when we attempt to bubble wrap their lives?

Do we paint bright red targets on our children's foreheads when bullies see their "mommies and daddies" chronically coming to the rescue?

Sometimes protecting and rescuing is the right thing to do.

When life and limb are in jeopardy...or excessive bullying is causing severe anxiety, depression, or other mental health problems...our kids need us to intervene.

An irony:

When we protect and rescue too much, it also places
our children at risk for developing severe anxiety,
depression, or other mental health problems.

Helicopter parenting sends a damaging unstated message to kids:

"You're too weak to cope with the problems you face. I'll have to do it for you."

What's most realistic?

Is it spending the lion's share of our time and energy trying to create a completely bullying-free world?

Might our time and other resources create a bigger positive impact if we help youth develop the skills and emotional strength required to cope with bullying?

What would happen if more young people knew how to peacefully strip bullies of their unhealthy power?

How do we move in this direction when the kids we know and love get bullied?

Consultant parents help their kids grow into capable, confident adults.

Instead of trying to solve all of their children's problems, they provide loving guidance and emotional support.

Consultant parents send a healthy unstated message:

"I love you and know that you are capable! You've got what it takes to make it in life!"

When their children experience bullying, consultant parents...

- Listen with great love and empathy.
- Get their children's perspective.
- Resist the urge to own the problem.
- Ask permission to share solutions.
- Offer sensible experiments.

Listen

There is nothing more important than an empathetic ear.

Glen shared his first reaction when his son, James, came home crying about being pushed around:

"My first thought was to call the school and give them a piece of my mind. How could they let this happen? I was irate!"

Glen continued:

"I also fantasized about telling James to knock 'em upside the head the next time it happened.

Fortunately, I remembered to shut my mouth and open my ears."

Glen resisted the urge to put on his drill sergeant uniform.

Glen also left his helicopter on the landing pad.

Wise parents don't throw away their drill sergeant or helicopter pilot skills.

They just save them for true emergencies.

First and foremost, kids experiencing bullying need an empathetic ear and an opportunity to vent.

The greatest gift is to listen and show that we care.

Why?

What happens when we try to "fix" someone else's problem? What happens when we fail to listen?

We invalidate their feelings and communicate that they are incapable of overcoming the challenges they face.

When we try too hard to fix our child's problems with bullies, we send the message that they are victims in need of rescuing, rather than victors who have the strength to face the inevitable hard knocks of life.

Listening also shows our kids that it's okay to visit with us when life feels painful and overwhelming.

James cried, "Those kids say I'm a stupid freak."

Hugging his son, Glenn replied, "I can't imagine how bad that must feel."

James was surprised but relieved by his father's brief yet compassionate reply.

"Yeah, and they do it all the time!"

Glenn answered, "And it happens all of the time? That must make it feel really bad."

Listening with empathy also opens our children's hearts and minds to the solutions we have to offer.

James's good and loving father was well on his way toward helping his son learn to face the challenge ahead.

Get their Perspective on Solutions

When we demonstrate interest in others' ideas, we communicate our belief that they can generate great ones.

Consultant parents send the unstated message:

"You are capable! I believe in you!"

Tiffany described why she guided her seven-year-old daughter toward thinking like a victor rather than a victim:

"I was so tempted to tell Abby what to do...but then I remembered what Love and Logic teaches."

Kids feel capable and competent only when seeing that they can cope with the challenges they face.

With a loving heart and careful guidance, we allow them to struggle with these challenges.

We help...but we try not to help too much.

Tiffany asked, "Abby, what do you think you might do to solve this problem?"

Drill sergeant parents say:

"Here's what you should do to solve this problem."

Helicopter parents say:

"Here's what I am going to do to solve your problem."

Consultant parents ask:

"What do you think you might do to solve this problem?"

Obviously, we don't expect our kids to have all of the answers, and we aren't shocked when they provide rather immature ones.

First grader, Abby, shared her ideas:

"I'm gonna kick him really hard. Then you could tell the principal to make the teachers watch kids closer so they can't be mean...or you could put me in a different school."

When our kids offer ideas, our job is to listen and to help them consider the possible consequences.

Tiffany replied, "I suppose that kicking him is one option. How would that work for you? Do you think that doing so would create an even bigger problem for you?"

Abby replied, "I'd get in trouble, too."

Mom answered with empathy, "Yeah, I think you're right."

Kids are far more likely to listen when they state the possible consequences of their solutions.

That's why consultant parents ask, "How would that work for you?"

Abby's eyes lightened as she pursued another avenue: "You could put me in a different school!"

Her mother replied with empathy, "I guess some people might try that. How would that work for you?"

Abby's smile disappeared. "But then I wouldn't see my friends."

Mom nodded. "That's true, and our family believes that it's usually best not to run away from our problems."

Mom continued, "Another idea you had was to talk to the principal. Would you like to hear some ideas about how you might ask her for help?"

Abby frowned. "You tell her to make those kids stop."

"Honey," Mom replied, "do you like being bossed around?"

Abby was adamant. "No!"

Mom smiled. "Do you think your principal will like it either?"

Abby walked just a bit taller as she and her mother left the principal's office. Asking for help wasn't as scary as she'd thought.

Resist the Urge to Own It

Our children can only learn from the challenges we allow them to own emotionally.

Because we love our kids so much, it's often difficult to see clearly when they're experiencing discomfort or pain.

When they scrape their knees, our knees tend to hurt.

When their hearts ache over bullying, our hearts also get achy.

Because we feel for them, it's easy to steal their opportunities to learn and feel strong.

Yes, it is tempting to own their struggles instead of allowing them to grow from them.

When we own their problems, our own feelings begin to rub off on them.

Donna relayed how she felt when her eleven-year-old Sarah, told her that some girls were refusing to sit with her at lunch:

"The pain was so intense I almost forgot I was no longer in middle school. It was as if I was the one being ostracized."

Donna also described how she made the transition from helicopter pilot to caring consultant:

"I realized, that for me, being a helicopter was really about trying to avoid the pain I felt when I was a kid. Now I had an opportunity to help my daughter by letting her have her own feelings...not mine."

Our kids take their emotional cues from us.

When we are fearful and anxious, they will be, too.

When we model calm confidence, we're more likely to see it in them.

Donna empathized with her daughter. "I know this is really, really hard. I also know that you are strong. What do you think you are going to do?"

Sarah shocked her mother with her self-assured response: "I guess that I really don't want to be friends with people who act that way."

Was Sarah's strength an accident, or was it inspired by the message communicated by her consultant parent mom?

When we believe our children can cope and solve problems, they believe they don't have to be traumatized by the bad manners, rudeness, and bullying of others.

Ask Permission to Share Some Solutions

Kids are more likely to accept our ideas when they know they don't have to.

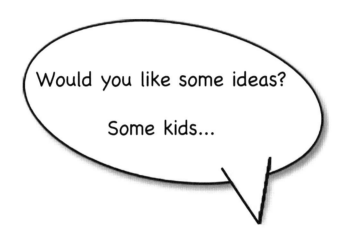

When it comes to dealing with the tougher challenge of bullying, kids typically need some significant help from adults.

How do we provide this help without constantly hearing, "That won't work!"?

Clint asked his sixteen-year-old the magic question:

"Would you like to hear what some people have experimented with?"

This question places kids in the driver's seat where they have a healthy sense of control.

"Would you like to hear what some people have experimented with?"

This question frames problem solving as an experiment rather than something the youth must do or try.

"Experimenting" is far less threatening than "doing" or "trying" something.

Sixteen-year-old Jesse replied, "I don't need you to tell me what to do."

Clint was in the perfect spot:

"I know. That's why I said **some people**. You get to decide."

Now Jesse was curious. "Well...what do they experiment with?"

Share Some Sensible Experiments

Experiments never fail. They simply move us closer to understanding what will work.

When it comes to solving tough problems like bullying, it's unwise to suggest that every experiment will work.

Why?

Kids are more likely to persevere when they understand that solving tough problems usually involves plenty of trial and error.

Wise parents provide only two or three "experiments" at a time, remembering to ask, "How will that work for you?" after each one.

The basic format is always the same:

"Some people (or kids) decide to experiment with
_____. How will that work for you?"

Experiment: Taking the Wind from their Sails

Bullies bully for a reason. For a few, it's material gain. These thugs twist arms and give snuggies for lunch money and other goodies.

Their numbers are few compared to the percentage who do it for emotional power and to cope with feelings of anger and hopelessness.

Their mission is accomplished when they see their victims cry, whine, scream, tattle, or attempt to retaliate in some way.

There is nothing that gives a bully more power than controlling the emotions of others.

Terrell's school counselor offered an experiment:

"Some kids decide to experiment with tricking those kids into thinking they aren't upset by the nasty things the bullies say. How might that work for you?"

She described what this looks like:

"Some kids decide to act calm and even a bit bored by the bully. Then they smile and say something silly like, 'Thanks for noticing', 'I know', or 'I was wondering about that.'"

Terrell also heard:

"Bullies like to feel powerful by making others upset. Sometimes they leave kids alone when they can't get that to happen. How do you think this might work for you?"

One week later:

A bully approached Terrell and said, "Your momma
_____."

Acting as cool as a cucumber, Terrell smiled, and said, "Yeah, I've been telling her to stop doing that stuff, but she just won't listen."

While the bully didn't give up entirely, it was clear that the wind had been stolen from his sails. It wasn't long before he found a more exciting victim.

Experiment: Standing Beside Your Allies

"Just walk away from the kid and tell an adult."

This has been the advice of many well-meaning drill sergeant parents.

The problem with this approach is that bullies follow.

They also become emboldened and bent on retribution when the victim turns tail and reports the problem in front of them.

Cole's parents provided a bit more sophisticated approach:

"Some kids decide to slowly move toward an adult or a group of nice kids. They do this without acting afraid and without letting the bully hear or see them tattling. How might that work for you?"

While it's certainly important for kids to report instances of bullying, it's equally important they do this at times when the bully is not immediately aware of it.

The effectiveness of standing beside one's allies hinges on the child's ability to act cool, move slowly, and not discuss the bullying incident until later when the bully is no longer present.

Experiment: Handling it with Strength

In some cases, bullying is best resolved by helping our kids see that sometimes respect is achieved by directly confronting the bully in a cool and collected manner.

Too frequently, a child develops a target on their back because they have a history of expecting adults to handle all of their peer problems.

"You need your mommy to protect you" is what bullies begin to believe about the child.

David introduced this experiment to his son, Joshua:

"Son, sometimes bullies only respect kids who show some real strength by letting them know that the way they are being treated just isn't acceptable."

David went on to say:

"Some kids decide to say to the bully, 'This is bullying, and it's got to stop! If it doesn't, I'm going to do something.' They do this by raising their voice just a little without acting really upset. How might that work for you?"

Did you notice the part about doing **something** if the bullying continues?

David explained "doing something" to his son...

"Some people decide to say they will do 'something' if the bullying doesn't stop. They do this because bullies are easier to deal with when they don't know what you are going to do."

David continued:

"When the bully asks, 'What are you going to do?'
some people decide to move toward an adult or
some of their friends."

Experiment: Changing One's Mind about being Bullied

Unfortunately, there are times when bullying can be incredibly difficult to stop...even for the most resourceful and confident kid.

Cyberbullying often falls into this category, largely because the perpetrators can hide behind their electronic devices and disseminate wide-range hurt in an instant.

Sometimes we cannot change our circumstances, but we can change our minds **about** our circumstances.

We all have some choices to make when being mistreated.

We can become bitter.

We can become vengeful.

We can believe the lies and view ourselves as worthless.

Or...

We can choose to see the bully as the weak, immature, or hurting person they are.

Our choice of thinking will make the difference.

Courtney was devastated by the slander being spread about her online. Her father shared an experiment:

"Some people decide to have a special reminder they say to themselves when they are feeling really low."

He added:

"Some people think, 'Those kids must be feeling really low.' Others say to themselves, 'If I start to believe what they say, they win.' Still others remind themselves, 'I'm glad I'm not that immature.' How might that work for you?"

Kids who are Strong Enough to Handle a Tough World

It all comes down to recognizing that we cannot create a stress- and conflict-free world for our children.

No matter how much we protect them, they will eventually face a world full of difficult, even dangerous, people...a world where rescue is not always possible.

Will they have the mental and emotional strength to survive?

Sure, but only if we allow the trials they face today to empower them in facing the more serious ones they will encounter tomorrow.

A gift to our kids:

Allowing them to learn life's hard lessons while still within our loving and protective reach.

Eleven-year-old Charlie was bullied by his fifth-grade teacher.

Nearly all of the teachers he'd met during his lifetime were caring and compassionate. She was not...she was a bully in every sense of the word.

Charlie's teacher believed a steady diet of criticism and public humiliation was the best way to handle students who wiggled in their seats and didn't complete their assignments.

In the small and remote community where Charlie and his family lived, there were no other fifth-grade classes and no other elementary schools.

Charlie was stuck with this teacher.

Dragging off of the school bus one afternoon, he lamented to his mother, "She's mean. She yells and tells me to stand in the corner."

Unbeknownst to Charlie, his mother was fighting the urge to tear this teacher limb from limb.

Instead of resorting to the violence she was beginning to consider, she empathized and listened.

Eventually, she shared some wisdom:

"Well...I guess the good thing, Charlie...is that you're going to get a lot of practice learning to make friends with difficult people. If you ever want some ideas, just let me know."

That year Charlie completed a comprehensive human relations training program...where he learned to build cooperative working relationships with neurotic and negative people.

Obviously, this course of study proved priceless as he grew older.

In fact, it was the most valuable course I ever took. Yes, I'm Charlie.

That wise woman was my mother.

When our children get bullied we always have the options of either piloting our helicopters or barking orders.

Sometimes these are the right options.

Whenever possible, however, doesn't it make sense to empower our children toward owning and solving the challenge?

Will they grow to feel happier and more confident as a result?

Thanks for reading!

Dr. Charles Fay

About the Author

Charles Fay, Ph.D. is a parent, author, and consultant to schools, parent groups, and mental health professionals around the world. His expertise in developing and teaching practical discipline strategies has been refined through work with severely disturbed youth in school, hospital, and community settings. Charles has developed an acute understanding of the most challenging students. Having grown up with Love and Logic, he also provides a unique...and often humorous...perspective.

More by Dr. Charles Fay

Real Talk on Technology

Parenting for Success

Stepparenting: Keeping it Sane!

Oh Great! What Do I Do Now?

From Bad Grades to a Great Life!

Technology and Kids

Love and Logic Events

Jim Fay and Charles Fay, Ph.D. present Love and Logic events and personal appearances for both parents and educators in many cities each year.

For more information, contact the Love and Logic Institute, Inc. at:
1-800-338-4065
or visit our website:
www.loveandlogic.com